WAR

HORSE

... BIOPICS

This is a
Phreestyle
Pholios
book

ISBN: 978-0-9569138-3-8

2011   Phreestyle Pholios, Alfriston,
East Sussex BN26 5XE

War Horse ... Biopics
makes understanding horses
in war very easy.

No prior knowledge of horses
is needed as salient points
are in the glossary.

The bite-size bios and illustrations
about the sacrifices and heroism of the
horse - man's partner through
the process of civilisation — will
move and inspire.

The small format has been chosen for
convenience — handbag size, the way
HM Queen Elizabeth II prefers her
Ascot Racecard!

TABLE OF CONTENTS

FEATURED HORSES

continued …

Front cover: Copenhagen and Wellington, Aldershot;
Back cover: Animal War Memorial, London
Photographer: Jane A Green

They say princes learn no art truly,
 but the art of horsemanship.
The reason is, the brave beast is no flatterer.
He will throw a prince as soon as his groom.

Ben Johnson
1573-1637

FOREWORD

For as long as there has been Man there has been war. Wars that have wreaked havoc not only on soldiers and the animals who served with them, but on civilians, livestock, wildlife and the cultures and landscapes of many continents.

From pre AD to the early days of World War II, horses have been significant in battle as the power to move equipment, stores and tents etc., as well as the mounts of officers, scouts and messengers.

The statistics are heart-breaking: the First World War took the lives of over eight million horses; in the Boer War of South Africa 300,000 died in less than three years; in the American Civil War one million perished.

But, amidst the bloodshed and the loss, some poignant and touching relationships were made demonstrating respect, trust, understanding and warmth, all testament to the unique — I do not use the word lightly — bond that can develop between *equus caballas* and *homo sapiens*, given the chance.

Horses put their trust in us, and we have to put our trust in them. We give them names just as we do ourselves and our pets. Training, riding or driving a creature that has many times our strength, is a fear-based prey animal with highly developed senses of hearing, sight and, not least, flight, takes a significant mutual confidence. To take that animal into terrifying situations such as battle and have that mutual trust working to mutual benefit, creates a special bond. A bond that, arguably, is betrayed by the brutal indiscriminate nature of warfare.

This book is not intended to be a missive on the equipment, strategy, dates or political purpose of warfare. Rather it is intended as a celebration of the war horse - whatever his battle, whatever his source, whoever he carried - by briefly telling the stories of some whose individual names or collective roles have been preserved in some way. We only wish we could cover them all.

~ ~ ~

Look back at our struggle for freedom,
Trace our present day's strength to its source;
And you'll find that man's pathway to glory
Is strewn with the bones of the horse.

Anon

INTRODUCTION

Respect and affection for the individual war horse is depicted in many monuments throughout many countries and social periods, though mostly as part of a memorial to his famous rider.

But the ordinary soldier who could not pay a grand tribute to his equine companion/s in battle still passed on some moving sentiments in diaries, poems - see *His Two Horses* and *A Soldier's Kiss* - and songs, such as Eric Bogle's *As If He Knows* telling of the heart-rending decision the soldiers made to personally shoot the horses that were not permitted to be returned to Australia and New Zealand rather than abandon them to a life of servitude.

Books, paintings, statues and monuments, as well as the unique play **War Horse**, and forthcoming film of same, all pay tribute to the heroic horse.

A key factor too in considering the plight of the war horse is that mostly the animals were requisitioned, removed from the home they knew and the people they trusted. They were taken regardless of their breed or type – anything that could work was off to the war.

For those not familiar with horses it is useful to remember that they come in breeds and types. For example, a lady's side-saddle mount would likely be a lightweight, refined, sensitive animal, whereas the plough horse would be heavy and strong but slow in movement and temperament – with many variations in between. All took their place in war.

Officers were mostly expected to provide their own mounts where possible, but often these were swapped from one to the other as the need arose.

Horses were required not only as the chargers of officers of cavalry, but to pull the gun carriages, form the supply chains and generally undertake the heavy-duty haulage work.

Mostly horses required in foreign fields were subjected to a journey by sea – a horrendous and often fatal experience as horses cannot vomit and suffer terribly from sea-sickness, not to mention the restricted accommodation and lack of vital exercise for the duration of the voyage – often a month or more. Many died en route.

The logistics of the conditions of warfare – lack of shelter and suitable food, impossible footing in times of heavy rain, bitter cold, unskilled handlers – all took even more of a toll on the horses, mules and donkeys, than did the fighting itself.

All in all war was a hell on earth for all involved whether they were on four legs or two.

~ ~ ~

BUCEPHALUS

There are many statues around the world depicting a youth
taming a horse – some say they are based on the story of
Alexander and Bucephalus.

BUCEPHALUS

Alexander the Great dreamt of a glorious life and everlasting fame. He achieved this – and so too did his loyal steed, **Bucephalus**.

Temperamental and dangerous, the gift horse to King Philip and been spurned as too unreliable for battle. The 12 year old Prince begged his father for a chance to ride him. Seeing his son's pride and confidence, reluctantly the King agreed. Alexander had noticed the horse was disturbed by shadows, so turned him into the sun before jumping up on his back. Boy and horse bonded instantly and from then on the black stallion was only ever ridden by Alexander who named him Bucephalus. Like the horses of the day he was small and stocky. Unlike the horses of the day he was treasured by perhaps the greatest general the world has ever seen.

At 20 Alexander was king and they campaigned together over 12 years and thousands of miles, the 'unreliable' horse never once failing the young King, even when confronting war elephants for the first time. Once, when he was stolen by marauders, Alexander would not move on until the horse was restored to him. When Bucephalus died, possibly at the age of 30, Alexander mourned him greatly. He had a city named after him which is the current site of Jelum in Pakistan. Unfortunately, the exact location of the interment of his remains is unknown and the statue that marked it has disappeared too, but, to compensate, other depictions of Bucephalus and his heroic owner are scattered around the world. Most will be familiar with the much reproduced ornament of a boy and a rearing horse - a depiction of the boy Alexander taming the stallion.

Scholars debate the final fate of Bucephalus, some supporting the theory that he died in battle; others saying this is unlikely as he was 30 when he died and that would be very old for a charger to still be going into combat. Some even think that the grief Alexander showed for his faithful steed was excessive and take it as proof of his perceived increasing 'madness'.

Of course, anyone who has ever had the experience of a true symbiosis of spirit with a wonderful horse will know the grief of the loss - when that horse has carried you into battle after battle and helped you conquer the known world, what sort of cretin would you be not to mourn him and wish to honour him as permanently as possible?

~ ~ ~

BABIECA

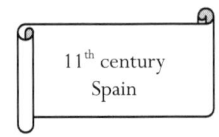

Instinct was the guide of the young Rodrigo Diaz de Vivar (later hailed 'El Cid') when he surveyed a herd of prospective war chargers. Despite the mutterings of his elders that the choice was stupid, he knew the ugly colt was the one for him. He bought him and named him **Babieca** which at that time meant 'stupid'. The horse proved to be far from stupid.

They were together through twenty years of battles and became legends in their time in the struggle to keep the Moors out of Spain. At one point, etiquette demanded that Rodrigo offer the horse to King Alfonso, but the King responded: "God forbid that I should take him. A horse like Babieca deserves no other rider than you, my Cid, so that together you may drive the Moors from the field and go to their pursuit. May God hide his favour from any who would take Babieca from you, for you and this horse have brought us great honour."

Even after his master's death Babieca could be trusted to convincingly obey Rodrigo's last orders. El Cid wanted his supported corpse, with sword upheld and visor open, to lead the cavalry into the breach of a final battle. His ploy worked, thanks to

the impeccable conduct of Babieca, as the enemy were so terrified that the warlord had risen from the dead that they scattered and were cut down as they ran in terror for their ships. Victory was won by a dead man and his noble horse.

Babieca died two years after El Cid and, in accordance with Rodrigo's request, was buried near him at the monastery of San Pedro de Cardeña. Two elm trees were planted to give the heroic horse shade. But later, to protect them in further troubled times, the family were exhumed and moved to the safer precincts of Burgos Cathedral. The sources now differ, some infer that Babieca was moved too and re-interred near the cathedral wall; others indicate he remained at the monastery. The statue of warrior and charger (featured on previous page) stands in the town square at Burgos, ancient capital of the region of Castile, Spain.

The grave of Babieca
is marked by this
headstone at the
Montastery of San Pedro
de Cardeña,
Spain

This magnificent head of Babieca stands in the grounds of what was the Olympic Stadium at Barcelona. The area is now a riding school but Babieca remains there in a corner next to a sheltering hedge.

GENGHIS KHAN

Oddly for a warrior of equestrian renown the name of any particular favourite horse of Genghis Khan has been obscured by the years. He utilised the local strong, swift, easy-gaited, enduring little Mongolian horses and his army consisted of 30,000 men each with two horses! In modern times the Mongolians have created a tribute to their ancient leader and his horsemanship which to date is the world's largest

equestrian statue, at a total height of over 50 meters. The body of the stainless steel horse contains conference rooms and it is possible to climb up inside and emerge between the horse's ears to enjoy the panoramic view of Mongolia.

SHARAD-NAR-AL-DIN

The golden war horse of the great Turkic warrior Tamarlane (1336-1405) whose name **Sharad-Nar-Al-Din** translates as 'My Golden Shadow'. When this horse was killed in battle Tamarlane vowed never to ride again.

~ ~ ~

SHARATZ

A pinto war horse of King Marko of the Empire of Serbia in the 14th century. The pair were known by the people as 'a dragon mounted on a dragon' and when King Marko died in 1399 **Sharatz** never allowed another person to ride him.

~ ~ ~

Fragments

In the 11th century BC, the funeral games of Patroklus after the Trojan War involved a five team chariot race, where the pair of horses driven by

Menelaos was a mare, Aithe and her harness partner, a stallion called Podargos. Achilles's own chariot horses were called Xanthos and Balios.

Britain's legendary King Arthur favoured **Llamrei**.

Prince Siddhartha (later Buddha) rode or drove **Kanthaka** in all the major events of his life including his escape from the palace to take up the life of an ascetic. When horse and Prince were parted, Kanthaka died of a broken heart.

Gazala was the horse of Baldwin I of Jerusalem, one of the leaders of the First Crusade. During the Crusade of 1101 Baldwin lost most of his army but escaped the Egyptians on his mare, Gazala.

Fauvel was the mount of King Richard I (the Lionheart) during the Crusades. Fauvel was a sorrel Arabian who was killed at the Battle of Jaffa (1192).

Britain's Queen Elisabeth I's mount of preference was her palfrey **Black Agnes**.

~ ~ ~

WHITE SURREY

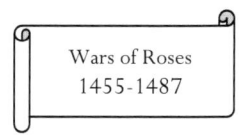

Wars of Roses
1455-1487

King Richard III was one of England's most notorious kings who met his end at the Battle of Bosworth in August 1485, the final battle of Britain's Wars of the Roses. Many legends surround both king and horse but one thing can be taken as certain and that is that **White Surrey** was the King's favoured war charger and he particularly chose him for the forthcoming battle.

In that final battle King Richard was unhorsed, separated from White Surrey in the melee, and ultimately killed. Schools taught their pupils that Richard lost his kingdom because he lost his horse and Shakespeare underlined this point in his play by giving a frantic and enraged king the lines "A Horse! A Horse! My Kingdom for a horse!"

White Surrey too, it is believed, lost his life on that battlefield but his valour is recorded in several paintings.

~ ~ ~

MATSUKAZE

Matsukze was the personal horse of the Japanese samurai Maeda Toshimasu, better known as Maeda Keiji. Matsukaze was extremely well bred but very wild of temperament. Only Toshimasu managed to tame him and the two became inseparable.

Matsukaze was a horse of immense strength, able to carry his large heavy master for days. The story goes that after Toshimasu died Matsukaze – living up to the meaning of his name Wind In The Pines - ran off and was never seen again.

STREIFF

Streiff (meaning Raider) was the horse of Gustavus Adolphus of Sweden who founded the Swedish

Empire which began the Golden Age of Sweden. He rode Streiff at the battle of Lützen in 1632. Streiff died at Wolgast in 1633; his hide was mounted on a wooden frame and has become the symbol of the Royal Armoury in Stockholm.

~ ~ ~

~ 16 ~

BLACKJACK

Oliver Cromwell overthrew the British monarchy and temporarily turned the country into a republic under his leadership. When his war charger **Blackjack** died, Cromwell had several 2ft tall

ceremonial jugs made from the hide. Shortly after this one (left) was deposited in a private bank and left there. It has been passed down the generations of the banking family and remains with descendants.

The insignia reads: "Oliver Cromwell Lord Protector of England, Scotland & Wales 1653". Blackjack was likely Cromwell's charger at the significant Battles of Marston Moor in 1644 and Naseby in 1645.

~ ~ ~

OLD DRUMMER

Jacobite Rebellion
1715

One of the earliest examples of a troop horse receiving honours was the survivor of the battle of Sheriffmuir in 1715. **Old Drummer** served with the King's Own Dragoons as a drum horse. Despite suffering a bullet in his neck he survived the battle and was ultimately retired to Teesdale. He lived to the amazing age of 45 years and the bullet was only extracted upon his death on 27th January 1753. He was interred in woodland at Snow Hall, Gainford, and the wooden plaque hung on a tree at the spot until the 1960s when it finally disintegrated. His obituary appeared in *The Gentleman's Magazine*, February 1753. His epitaph revealed that 'he never lik'd the rattling of a drum, and always dreaded the firing of a gun', and that his civilian life was spent first as a lady's horse and then in farm work …

Which he well perform'd till with old age oppress'd
In Great content enjoy'd some years of rest.
Yesterday he was the oldest horse alive,
Today he's dead, and aged 45.

~ ~ ~

NELSON

George Washington's equestrian statue in DC often draws the question from tourists "What's his horse's name?" Washington had several horses that are named in the record: Blueskin, a bluish white horse that wasn't partial to gunshots; Magnolia and Lindsay's Arabian. He bred horses and rode to hounds but for battle his favourite was Nelson who was a reliable and courageous war horse, so presumably it is **Nelson** depicted in the statue by Thomas Crawford on Capitol Hill. Nelson survived

the rigors of near starvation and punishing marches from Boston to the Carolinas.

Both Nelson and Blueskin retired to Washington's home at Mt Vernon where they were kept in the well fed comfort they had earned.

~ ~ ~

DUKE

The horse ridden by General Andrew Jackson when he triumphed over the British at the Battle of New Orleans was **Duke**. He was kept in retirement by Jackson who is on record as sighing "Ah poor fellow, we have seen hard times together, we must shortly separate, your days of suffering and toil are well-nigh ended." The statue by Clark Mills is significant for two reasons: it was the first bronze statue cast in America (1853) and was the first equestrian statue in the world depicting a horse balanced on his hind legs.

Washington DC has the original statue, three more were cast with the one depicted here being in

Lafayette Square, New Orleans (1856); the others are in Nashville, Tennessee (1880) and Jacksonville, Florida (1987).

BROWN BEAUTY

Though not a war horse in the sense of going into battle – as far as we know – **Brown Beauty** takes her place in the annals of war because she was 'borrowed' by Paul Revere for his 'great ride' to warn that the "British are coming", an event also immortalised in a poem by HW Longfellow.

This statue stands in Boston, Massachusetts and was sculpted by Cyril Dallin.

COPENHAGEN

was the favourite war charger of the Duke of Wellington, throughout the Peninsula Wars and at the Battle of Waterloo, when the Duke was in the saddle for over eighteen hours. Yet the horse was still spirited enough to kick when patted. "I have never seen a horse with such bottom" the Duke remarked proudly - meaning there's no end to his strength or spirit.

Copenhagen was so named as his dam (the mount of Lord Grosvenor) made the trip to Copenhagen to capture the Danish fleet in the harbour. When she was found to be in foal she was returned home to Grosvenor's Thoroughbred breeding facility and her foal was born in 1808.

When the battles were done, Copenhagen came back with the Duke to Stratfield Saye for a long and happy retirement, even giving rides to the grandchildren and others - presumably his temper had calmed somewhat by then!

When he died in 1836 at the age of 28, he was interred with full military honours at Stratfield Saye, where his grave can still be visited today under the Turkey Oak at the Ice House. The Duchess wore a bracelet of his hair and the Duke refused to have him exhumed in order for his skeleton to be displayed alongside Marengo's in the Museum.

A statue of the Duke on Copenhagen was installed at London's Hyde Park Corner but in 1885, due to the pressures of traffic, both the commemorative Arch and statue had to be relocated.

The future King Edward VII thought it appropriate that the statue be placed in Aldershot (the home town of the British Army), where it still presides today on Round Hill near to the Garrison Church (see front cover).

The inscription at the bottom of the grave marker

stone at Stratfield Saye, Hampshire, reads:

"God's humbler instrument,
though meaner clay
Should share the glory of
that glorious day."

~ ~ ~

MARENGO

Napoleon Bonaparte had a passion for grey Arabian stallions which he always chose to use for battle, often naming them after his battles: Jaffa, Wagram, Austerlitz and of course **Marengo**. Another of his grey Arabian stallions, Le Vizier, is mounted and on display at the Musée de l'Armée in Paris.

However, much as he enjoyed riding – often going off for a gallop – Napoleon was a poor rider. He pointed his toes down, and slouched and slipped about in the saddle – so much so that he wore holes in his breeches! As a consequence his horses had to be rigorously trained to make them steady enough for him. They were subjected to shots near their heads, dogs and pigs running through their legs, drums and trumpets suddenly sounding, flags waving and swords and bayonets slashing around them. He preferred his horses to be 'easy amblers' this being a long-prized but now mostly forgotten smooth saddle gait.

Marengo joined Napoleon in 1799 after the Battle of Aboukir in Egypt and also rode him in the Battle of Austerlitz in 1805 and during the long haul to Moscow and back in 1812. Depicted in the famous painting by Jacques Louis David of Napoleon Crossing the Alps, the image does not convey the fact that at the time of this 3,000 mile trek Marengo was aged 19.

At the Battle of Waterloo on 18th June 1815 Napoleon rode Marengo all day. Clad in all his finery of red and gold shabraque and gold-plated bit and buckles, Marengo eventually took several wounds in his hip which disabled him sufficiently that he had to be abandoned. One of Wellington's officers rescued him and brought him to England where he was taken to the hearts of the people and became a celebrity. When paraded in Pall Mall in London in 1823 thousands of people thronged to see him. He still had visible scars of his five wounds and, less visibly, a bullet was permanently lodged in his tail.

Ultimately he was sold and went to stud at Ely. When in 1832 he died at 39 years old, Marengo's skeleton was articulated and is still on display at the National Army Museum in Chelsea; his hooves were made into snuff boxes and one is at St James's Palace, London.

~ ~ ~

TANNAR

TANNAR

The mount of Colonel Edward Cheney, **Tannar** was one of four killed under him at the Battle of Waterloo.

It is believed to be the only full size equestrian statue in an English church. Originally located at nearby Gaddesby Hall, Leicestershire, UK, the statue was moved to the parish church in 1917 but according to

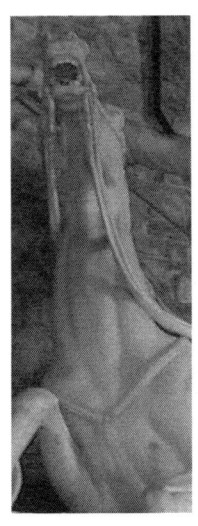

the architect Pevsner is of "a type more suited for St Paul's Cathedral".

Tannar's teeth are blackened from having an apple inserted into his mouth at each Harvest Festival. The sculptor, Joseph Gott, is said to have been distraught to discover he had failed to give Tannar a tongue. The alabaster statue clearly depicts the fatal bullet wound in Tannar's chest.

~ ~ ~

LISETTE was a very fierce, aggressive horse who seemed set on revenge. Her story was preserved in the memoirs of her owner, a captain of Napoleon's chasseurs, General Baron de Marbot. In combat a bayonet aimed at Marbot missed and ripped into the mare's thigh. She promptly retaliated by lunging at the offending grenadier and with one bite took off his facial skin along with his nose, lips and eyebrows. She then launched into a general attack, kicking and striking at everyone. Grabbing a Russian by his stomach, she lifted him off his feet and carried him off to a nearby hill where, once his entrails were ripped out, smashed him under her feet in the snow. Her rider managed to stay in the saddle but obviously had no control over her. She galloped back to base, arriving exhausted, all her blood having pumped out of her severed vein, and collapsed. But she recovered and after a swift lesson about biting involving a sizzling piece of roast mutton, she became more amenable and ultimately retired in 1807 to become a delightful ladies' hack. She died of old age some eight years later.

~ ~ ~

BLAKE

The Thoroughbred charger of Colonel Kerrison had carried his rider through the whole Peninsula campaign, even though wounded, and was one of the few sent on the return journey home. But the ship that carried him and some of his comrades was wrecked near the Lizard, at the tip of Cornwall, UK, and all were drowned.

~ ~ ~

JACK

On 20 June 1836 the last surviving equine warrior of the 'Hundred Days War' was euthanized at Knightsbridge Barracks, at the age of 27 and buried in Hyde Park, London. 'Waterloo Jack' on each anniversary of the battle had been decked with laurels and proudly paraded at the head of the Regiment. His duties were done.

~ ~ ~

Fragment from Napoleon

"How do we know that animals have not a language of their own? My opinion is that it is a presumption in us to say no, because we do not understand them. A horse has memory, knowledge and love"

~ ~ ~

PALOMO

Palomo was Simón Bolívar's foremost war charger in Latin America's successful struggle for independence from Spain. Palomo accompanied Bolívar on most of his national liberation campaigns. The horse was light grey, tall, with a tail that reached the ground and Bolívar named him Palomo, which meant cock pigeon. The horse was a gift to him from an elderly peasant woman from Santa Rosa de Viterbo, Boyacá Department, shortly before the Battle of Boyacá in 1819. Bolívar lent Palomo to one of his officers, but the horse died from exhaustion after an extremely harsh long distance march. He was buried near to a chapel close to a very old ceiba tree. Palomo's shoes and other effects of Bolívar are on exhibit in the Museum of Mulaló, Columbia.

~ ~ ~

MEEANEE

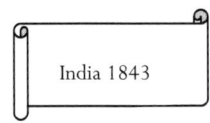

India 1843

In 1843 one of the decisive battles of the Conquest of the Scinde (coastal area of India in what is now Pakistan) was the battle of Meeanee which was successful for the British. The cavalry horse, now bearing the name **'Meeanee'** to honour his participation in that battle, was to become the mount of Governor General Henry Hardinge, then Commander-in-Chief of the Forces, later Viscount. When he returned to his home at South Park in Penshurst, Kent, UK, Meeanee came too.

Viscount Hardinge died in 1856 but Meeanee had preceded him, coming to the end of his colourful life under a yew tree at South Park, which became his gravesite and where he still lies.

In 1857 John Foley's 19ft tall statue of Hardinge mounted on his grey Arabian stallion, was erected in Calcutta, but eventually became the rallying point of insurgents. Lady Hardinge purchased the statue from the Indian government in the early 1960s and arranged its shipment home where it stood in front

MEEANEE

of the house at South Park for 20 years until about 1985 when the family sold the property.

A family member wrote a 26-line poem *Lines On Meeanee's Grave* which included the sentiment:

> .... Untouched himself, the steed his master bore
> In safety, midst the thunderbolts of war,
> And when the Lord in empire's care resigned
> Kept by a soldier's sword and stateman's mind
> The faithful charger followed as a friend,
> To share the joys these homely haunts attend.
> To end, in honour far from scenes of strife
> The closing days of an eventual life
> And dying – stretched beneath this Yew Tree's shade
> Those sinewy limbs that ne'er their trust betrayed.

The statue is now in the garden of the home of a descendant in a village in Cambridgeshire (previous page) and Meeanee's tail and hoof are preserved in the Museum in Maidstone, Kent.

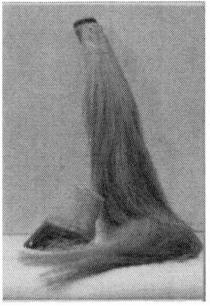

RONALD

Crimean War
1853-1856

Cannon to right of them,
Cannon to left of them,
Cannon behind them
Volley'd and thunder'd;
Storm'd with shot and shell,
While horse and hero fell,
They that had fought so well
Came thro' the jaws of Death
Back from the mouth of Hell,
All that was left of them,
Left of six hundred
When can their glory fade?
O the wild charge they made!
All the world wondered.
Honour the charge they made,
Honour the Light Brigade,
Noble six hundred.

The famous poem by Alfred Lord Tennyson tells a vivid story of an incredible episode in British history, the Charge of the Light Brigade at the Battle of Balaklava in the Crimean War. The date October 25, 1854, and the name of the 7th Earl of Cardigan at the head of the 13th Light Dragoons, are well known milestones of history to schoolboy and historian. The steed that carried James Thomas Brudenell 'into the mouth of Hell' was **Ronald**, a chestnut with white socks, 15.2hh, who had been bred at the Brudenell family seat, Deene Park in Northamptonshire. Selected as his personal cavalry charger for the Charge, it fell to Ronald to hear the Earl's legendary words "Here goes the last of the Brudenells" as they galloped at the head of the Brigade into battle – an attack that was ordered by superior officers and disapproved of by Cardigan.

Soon, as Brudenell had predicted, the Light Brigade was bombarded from three sides, one shell narrowly missing the heroic Ronald. Outraged, Cardigan suddenly spurred to a gallop and charged through the guns and on through the Russian cavalry and infantry. Thus perceiving that he had fulfilled the orders to which he had so strongly objected, he wheeled Ronald around and sped back along the valley. Somehow, perhaps due to the valour and reliability of Ronald, the Earl emerged unscathed from the jaws of Death. When at last the Light

Brigade withdrew over the bodies of their hundreds of fallen, the cost was counted: of the 673 only 195 men and horses were still fit for duty, the rest killed or horribly wounded. No less than 475 horses were killed in that one legendary battle and many more were never to see England again. Fortunately, Ronald was not one of them.

Once home they could not rest as people thronged around Ronald trying to grasp little pieces of hair as remembrances at parades.

Outliving the Earl, who died of an accident with another horse, Ronald's last service to Cardigan was to follow the coffin in his funeral cortege. However, the old horse, having endured ghastly sea journeys, life on the foreign front, the atrocity of battle, near starvation and probably deep terror, found the whole prospect of a funeral procession far too exhilarating and became boisterous. To avoid the solemn pageantry of the day being ruined by the over-excited horse, they administered laudanum. But, in the heat of the moment the dose must have been inadvertently overdone, for then no one could

Ronald's head preserved at Deene Park

move the dozing charger. Eventually an inspired individual called for the sounding of the cavalry charge. Stirred to duty, Ronald jumped into wakefulness and set off as required.

Four years later, on June 28, 1872, Ronald died. The Brudenell family honoured the valiant old horse by preserving his tail and his head at the family country seat in Northamptonshire.

To this day, in the White Hall, he gazes upon the daily sightseers to the historic Deene Park House. Ronald's splendid contribution to British history has not only been recorded in poetry, but in two films and several magnificent paintings.

~ ~ ~

EXQUISITE was heralded the handsomest animal in the Crimea and was the mount of Lord George Paget, an officer in the second line of the Charge of the Light Brigade.

~ ~ ~

OLD BOB

Alongside the glamorous chargers of the Crimea worked troop horses, one of which was **Old Bob**. He became the mount of the farrier-major who rode him throughout the Crimean campaign. Old Bob was never sick or sorry for himself, survived the Charge and the rigours of that Crimean winter to return safely to Britain with his regiment. Retired in Cahir, County Tipperary, he died in 1862, buried with full military honours and a tombstone was erected in his memory. The plaque below can be found set in the wall at the Library.

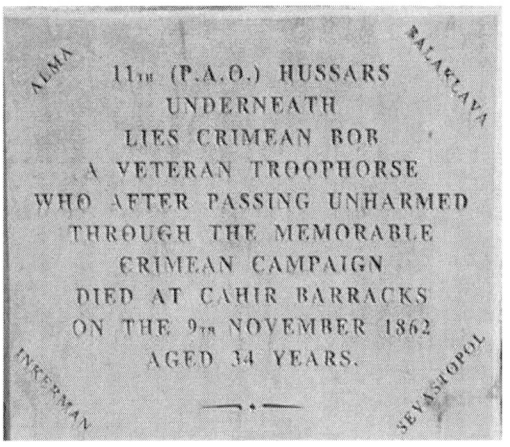

SIR BRIGGS

Sir Briggs was purchased by Godfrey Morgan, Viscount Tredegar, in 1851, the year he won the hunt Steeplechase at Cowbridge in Wales.

In 1854 he was shipped out to the Crimea and was one of the few out of the forty aboard who survived the voyage. Playing his part in the Charge of the Light Brigade, Sir Briggs received a sabre cut to his head. But he survived the melee and, when Godfrey became sick and was returned to Constantinople, Sir Briggs was used as a staff horse by the Viscount's brother, Frederick Morgan. In the same year as Sebastopol fell, Sir Briggs won a military steeplechase there.

Ultimately Sir Briggs was returned to Tredegar House, Wales, in 1855 and lived to be 28 years of age, dying on 6th February 1874.

Godfrey was always attributing his own safe return from the Crimea to the valour of his horse, and when eventually Sir Briggs died he honoured him by having him buried in the cedar garden at Tredegar House, where a monument stands to this day.

At Tredegar there is a painting of Sir Briggs at the Charge of the Light Brigade and nearby one of his shoes frames a photograph of Godfrey in his later years.

Sir Briggs's memorial reads:

"He carried his master the Hon. Godfrey Morgan, Captain 17th Lancers, boldly and well at the Battle of Alma, in the first line of the Light Cavalry Charge at Balaclava and the battle of Inkerman, 1854."

Another tribute is the equestrian statue by Sir
William Goscombe John (1909) at the
City Hall in Cardiff

SIR BRIGGS

~ ~ ~

I'd rather have a goddam horse.
A horse is at least human, for God's sake.
J.D. Salinger

BUTCHER – The Balaklava Mare

War horses perform many duties and one mare, **Butcher**, became the mount of the all-important trumpeter of the 13th Light Dragoons at the Charge of the Light Brigade. For easy recognition trumpeters were usually mounted on grey horses, but by this time there were none left and Butcher, a tall bay, was promoted. Imagine the trust horse and bugler had to have in each other as they faced the blasting Russian guns. It is often said that horses do not feel fear in these situations as long as they feel a familiar hand on the reins and the weight of their rider on their backs. Who knows?

Butcher was shot in the right fore leg but did not falter. It was a further two years before that war ended and Butcher was shipped home with just 44 of the other surviving horses. She landed at Portsmouth, was inspected by Queen Victoria, and that very evening was shipped off again to Ireland. She served for a further 17 years including a spell in Canada! Eventually retiring in 1873, she was the last living survivor of the Charge of the Light Brigade – Ronald having died a year before. The Queen accepted Butcher as a gift and she was kept in comfort at Windsor until, at about age 30, she died.

~ ~ ~

VONOLEL

Lord Roberts was carried by **Vonolel** through the two years campaigning of the Second Afghan War and also on the famous 320 mile forced march from Kabul to Kandahar, which was accomplished in just 21 days. He was a purebred Arabian stallion from the desert who found himself imported to Bombay and purchased by Lord Roberts in 1878. He was grey, about 14.3 hands, and quite happy with his owner's weight as Lord Roberts was only ten stone.

Vonolel returned home with Roberts in 1893 and in 1897 was ridden by him behind Queen Victoria's carriage in her Diamond Jubilee procession. The crowds were delighted. On his breastplate Vonolel wore the honours presented to him by the Queen herself, the Kandahar Star and the Afghan Medal. When he died two years later he was given a military funeral and was buried in the Rose Garden at the Royal Hospital in Kilmainham, Dublin. Part of the epitaph on his grave marker reads:

> There are men both good and wise
> Who hold that in a future state
> Dumb creatures we have cherished here below
> Shall give us joyous greeting when
> We pass the golden gate
> Is it folly that I hope it may be so?

~ ~ ~

MAIDAN

Another purebred Arabian stallion to 'land on his hooves' after Afghanistan, was **Maidan** (a name meaning large open field). He was bought by Captain Johnstone of the Indian Army and had raced with some success as a three-year old. Then he was sold to Lt Col Brownlowe who weighed 19 stone but though only small, the 14.3hh Arabian carried him without fuss throughout the Afghan campaigns and on the Kabul-Kandahar March. When he was fourteen he passed to Captain Vesey of the 9th Lancers. Posted home in 1885, Vesey took Maidan with him, pausing on route to race the horse against the fine Arabians of the French Government Stud. When he died the horse passed to a Miss Dillon who founded one of the earliest Arabian studs in England. Still up to his duties the old stallion sired a number of fine Arabians who were among the first to be exported to America. At age 20 Maidan won many point-to-point races against Thoroughbreds and at 22 won a three-mile steeplechase. He was euthanized after breaking a leg.

~ ~ ~

DICK, BLACK PRINCE and CLOWN

These chargers had the distinction of belonging to Britain's Lord Baden-Powell.

Black Prince was presented to him by the people of Australia. His second horse was **Clown**, who was a happy fellow, except when the hair around his hooves needed trimming. He would kick and fight so much that once it was only achieved because he knocked himself out on a wall and was unconscious for the duration!

Dick had been taught many circus tricks before the war and could be totally trusted to do what most would not and that was to stand alone and wait for his absent rider's return.

~ ~ ~

When you are on a great horse, you have the best seat you will ever have.
Sir Winston Churchill

MILITARY HORSE GRAVES
Aldershot, Hampshire, UK

The "**Cemetery for Famous Old Horses**" contains five graves tucked between the golf fairway and Shoe Lane, amid ferns, beech, silver birch and fir trees. Shaded by russet leaves, the graves are rather neglected and the inscriptions eroded but they are engraved as follows:

1. To mark the spot where the **Grey Horse** is buried which was ridden throughout the South African war by Lt Gen Sir John French ...
2. Do not disturb the bones of **Princess**, who served in Her Majesty's Army for 21 years until she ended her days as first charge to Lt General Sir Archibald Alison Bart CCB, commanding the Aldershot Division, and was laid here 6th December 1888 aged 26 years
3. **Jock** died March 29th 1899
4. **Polly** died September 8th 1885
5. Here rests **Fatima**, better known as Fatty the favourite pony of HRH Princess Patricia of Connaught, died July 18th during the command of General HRH The Duke of Connaught.

As yet, I have been unable to find out more about these interments, except that before the days of the golf course the location was part of Government House gardens.

TRAVELLER

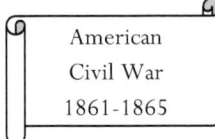

American
Civil War
1861-1865

Confederate General Robert E Lee and his horse
Traveller were icons of the American Civil War,
winning the affection of the soldiers and civilians of
both sides. In General Lee's words about a possible
painting of the horse: "Such a picture would inspire
a poet, whose genius could then depict his worth
and describe his endurance of toil, hunger, thirst,
heat and cold, and the dangers and suffering and
dilate upon his sagacity and affection, and his
invariable response to every wish of his rider. But I
am not an artist and can only say he is a Confederate
Gray."   Traveller retired with Lee and they often
rode out together from their base in Richmond,
Virginia, which is now Lee University. Lee would
say Traveller was "my only companion, I may say
my only pleasure". Traveller outlived the General by
a number of years and marched in his master's
funeral procession, his step slow and head bowed
exactly as if he knew the meaning of the occasion.
He was a tourist attraction in his own right, but in
1871 he died of tetanus due to a nail wound in his
hoof. He was buried at Lee University, Lexington,
Virginia, and visitors still throw coins on the marker
stone for good luck, just as they once plucked hairs

from his mane or tail. A full length very moving novel by Richard Adams tells *Traveller*'s story in the first person.

The 50ft monument of Lee and Traveller,
sculpted by Jean Antoine Mercie, was unveiled in
Monument Avenue, Richmond, in 1890,and forms the
centre of the traffic roundabout.

HERO

The vigorous statue by Gary Casteel of **Hero** and General Longstreet magnificently captures the tension of battle.

Hero was Longstreet's mount at the disastrous Battle of Gettysburg and their statue is in Pitzer Woods. It captures the energy of the horse in a stunning moment of great action and strain as he throws himself into obeying his rider's body command to spin to the left. The whole effect is enhanced by the fact that it is not on a plinth but directly on the ground.

The statue was the last to be dedicated in the Gettysburg Military National Park (1998).

VIRGINIA

The flamboyant General J.E.B. Stuart was said to favour the mare **Virginia** and rode her in many of his dashing campaigns.

The story goes that it was her valiant leap of an enormous ditch that saved him out of the jaws of potential capture by the Union Army. The horses of the Commander of the Cavalry were particularly vulnerable in both combat and reconnaissance and all Stuart's were fatally wounded in action.

Sculptor Frederick Moynihan; statue unveiled May 1907 in Monument Avenue, Richmond, Virginia.

BLACK BESS

Black Bess was the favoured mount of the *Thunderbolt of the Confederacy*, General John Hunt Morgan, who led the famed 'Morgan's Raiders' and was a pivotal figure in the Civil War. The Raiders were a swift moving, hard hitting cavalry mounted exclusively on the prototype Saddlebred horses.

They were a popular pair and when they stopped at settlements the women and children would rush to greet them and take snippets of Bess's mane and tail hair for keepsakes.

The statue stands outside the History Museum in Lexington, Kentucky and the General is buried nearby. The inscription on the statue reads:

"General Hunt Morgan and his Bess"

The gorgeous horse portrays all the qualities of her type, but for some reason the sculptor, Pompeo Coppini, felt that the General should not be depicted on a mare, so added parts that changed her gender! Such nonsense.

~ ~ ~

LITTLE SORREL

The favoured mount of General 'Stonewall' Jackson even though she was so small his feet nearly touched the ground. He valued her for her toughness, courage, stamina and smooth gait, utilising her endurance to the degree that his staff often requested a slower pace as their horses were exhausted. When Jackson was killed by friendly fire, she was captured and then returned to

the rebel army, only to be captured again and returned again.

After the war she participated in many fairs and reunions including the New Orleans World Fair in 1885. But her health started to deteriorate and she was kept standing by the aid of a sling which tragically slipped one day and she crashed to the ground breaking her back. Her hide was mounted and is at the Virginia Military Institute in Lexington and her remains were buried at the foot of the Jackson monument in Richmond.

RED EYE

Brig. Gen. Richard B. Garnett initially rode a dark bay mare who was killed early in the battle of Gettysburg. For Pickett's Charge, to the horror of his fellows, he mounted his best horse, **Red Eye**, a black gelding – he would be the only mounted combatant in the charge and thus easy pickings for the Union fire. But he could not be dissuaded.

Horse and rider went down in a hail of lead near the stone wall. Half an hour later, the riderless Red Eye came running back across the Confederate lines a deep wound in his shoulder and so panicked that he jumped over crouching soldiers on the way. Unusually for an officer of such standing, the General's body was never recovered and it was assumed that the canister was shot so close to him that he was unrecognisable and consequently was mistakenly buried in one of the mass graves. How Red Eye survived such a blast is a mystery.

~ ~ ~

Fragment

Union General Carter wrote: *"The sight of General Lee and his splendid warhorse, Traveller, was a graven image in the heart of every red blooded soldier"*

~ ~ ~

CINCINNATI

Sculptors: Henry Shrady and Edmund Amateis.

Cincinnati was General Ulysses S. Grant's favourite war horse and was given to Grant as a gift from an admirer in 1864. He was a 17hh chestnut by the famous racehorse Lexington, the fastest four-miler at the time. Grant reckoned he was the finest horse he had ever seen and was not keen to let others ride him. The exceptions were his old school chum Admiral Ammen and President Abraham Lincoln, the latter rode Cincinnati every day whilst visiting with Grant.

Grant rode Cincinnati throughout the war and to the surrender meeting with General Lee at the Appomattox, when, being a superb horseman himself and respecting the courage and stamina of the horses of the Deep South, Grant gave the Confederate cavalry permission to take their horses home with them.

At war's end Cincinnati and Grant were not separated and the horse moved to the White House too, and ultimately retired to the farm of Admiral Ammen in Maryland where he died in 1878.

Set on a long marble platform in Capitol Hill, Washington DC, the General and Cincinnati stand proud in the centre, surrounded by bronzes of cavalry, artillery and four lions. Under construction for eight years the monument was dedicated in 1922.

BALDY

The horse of Union General George Meade was held in high esteem by this rather grumpy senior officer who often wrote of him in his letters home to his wife.

It was **Baldy** he rode at the Battle of Gettysburg when his forces won the day against Lee's Confederates. Baldy had been wounded on many occasions including being left for dead at Antietam, but was later found grazing with a deep wound in his neck. He was nursed back to health and eventually Meade retired him. He was to outlive the general by ten years and participated in his funeral as the traditional riderless horse. When he died himself in 1882 he was buried at Downington, Pennsylvania. However, a few days later two veterans of the war succumbed to nostalgia and dug him up, removed his head and took it back to their post where to this day it presides over the Philadelphia Civil War Library Museum in a steel reinforced glass case. The Old Baldy Civil War Round Table of Philadelphia still commemorate him and regard him with reverence.

~ ~ ~

OLD WHITEY

This modest glacial stone marks the last resting place of an honoured old war horse.

On March 20th 1879, at the White House President Rutherford B. Hayes was handed a four-word message: "Old Whitey is dying."

Before the evening was out, a second telegram arrived from his family home at Fremont, Ohio, notifying the president that, indeed, his beloved war horse had breathed his last. Despite every veterinary effort he had succumbed to spinal meningitis at age 29 having dodged the artillery aimed at him in 19 battles during the war – being a light grey he was a prime target. Such was his reputation that when the war was declared over, Rebel soldiers asked to see 'the big white horse' that they had 'fired at ten thousand times'. Hayes would proudly bring him out for them to admire.

Old Whitey was mascot of the 23rd Ohio Volunteer Infantry. He died in 1879 and was buried at the Hayes family estate, Spiegel Grove, with the marker declaring *Old Whitey A Hero of Nineteen Battles 1861-1865.*

He was interred "like a warrior taking his rest with hay and his blanket around him" and lies not far from his cavalry officer-cum-US President Hayes who was ultimately re-interred back in Spiegal Grove, Fremont, Ohio.

~ ~ ~

WINCHESTER

Gen. Philip Sheridan's black horse **Reinzi** carried him on his desperate ride from Winchester to Cedar Creek in the Shenandoah Valley, and in memory of that event was renamed **Winchester**.

After the war Sheridan submitted an official record of the horse's service in which he pointed out his "great intelligence, immense strength and endurance ... I doubt his superior as a horse for field service was ever ridden by anyone". Later, Winchester's stuffed body was on display at the Army Museum but when that suffered a fire, he was removed to the Smithsonian Museum where he is still on display. This statue is at Fort Sheridan, Illinois. The 'Ride' is also depicted in a magnificent painting by Thure de Thulstrup (1848-1930) and in a poem by Thomas Buchanan Read:

"...Here is the steed that saved the day
By carrying Sheridan into the fight,
From Winchester twenty miles away!"

SAM

Union General W.T. Sherman and his horse **Sam** made one of the longest marches in the war from Vicksburg, Mississippi, through the Deep South to Washington. The big bay horse received many wounds, once being shot right through the neck, but he didn't waiver, just carried on calmly. When at last the war was over, Sherman retired the horse to a friend's farm in Illinois, where he happily became the mount of the children. Eventually dying of extreme old age in 1884, he was interred on the farm but the place is now lost having been given over to a housing

estate. The town of Frankfort, Illinois, commemorates its connection with Sam with a metal statue by Margi Hafer, depicting the old horse with the children and Sherman.

FANCY

Major General John Reynolds of the Union Army was a highly respected officer and exemplary horseman, mounted, it is recorded, on the superb elegant black horse, **Fancy**.

On the very first day of Gettysburg he was shot in the neck and fell from Fancy and died. Fancy was then ridden by an orderly who dragged the General from the field.

The statue is at Gettysburg; the sculptor was Henry Kirk Bush-Brown.

Those horses with statues or monuments were not the only ones that played their part in this long, gruelling, bloody war.

General Lee's other horses included **Lucy Long**, **Richmond**, **Brown-Roan** and **Ajax**.
Sherman also rode **Duke**, **Dolly**, and **Lexington**.
Grant also rode: **Jack**, **Kangaroo**, **Fox**, **Jeff Davis**, **Rondy** and **Methuselah**.
J.E.B. Stuart: **My Maryland**, **Highfly**.
General Sickles: **Grand Old Canister**.
Ewell: a flea-bitten gray called **Rifle**.
Custer: **Don Juan**, **Harry**, **Dan Vic** and **Roanake**.
Hooker's horse was **Lookout**.
Colonel Alexander: **Dixie**.
Trimble's horse was **Jinny**. As they crossed the Emmitsburg Road, a bullet smashed the General's left ankle, also wounding Jinny. Bravely, Jinny managed to safely return the General to the Confederate lines but subsequently died of her own wounds.
Colonel Chamberlain: **Charlemagne**.
The war horse of Major General John Sedgwick, commander of the VI Corps was **Handsome Joe**. Surviving Gettysburg unharmed, General Sedgwick was killed ten months later at the battle of

Spotsylvania Court House. He was the highest-ranking Union casualty in the entire Civil War. A statue just north of Little Round Top depicts General Sedgwick sitting atop Handsome Joe. The general's other horses included **Rambler** and **Cornwall**.

Rolla, an 18hh bay and **Washington**, a bright sorrel, were both horses of Gen Winfield Scott.

Grey Eagle was the "old white horse" of Brigadier. General. John Buford, commander of the 1st Division, Cavalry Corps. Gen. Buford died, probably of typhoid, in Washington D.C. five months after the battle of Gettysburg. Grey Eagle participated in his master's funeral procession which was also attended by President Lincoln.

One of Stonewall Jackson's staff recalled the death of his horse in his memoirs. **Dick Turpin** was wounded at Cedar Creek, one bullet in his leg, a second in his jaw. He "gave a weird cry of pain, sprang into the air, reared straight up, and throwing his head back in agony struck me in the face and knocked me from the saddle". But, blood pouring from his mouth, he galloped through the enemy column and in the dark negotiated a deep ravine and took them both back to safety, where he collapsed. Two days later he died of lockjaw (tetanus).

COMANCHE

General Custer's forces were annihilated by 3,000 Sioux and Cheyenne warriors at the Battle of the Little Big Horn in 1876. Three hundred and nineteen horses perished that day but, when the relief column arrived, they found one buckskin gelding still standing amid the carnage, **Comanche**. He had been so named for his stoic service in a previous battle when he had continued to fight on with the shaft of an arrow embedded in his quarters. Comanche's survival of the Little Big Horn confrontation is something of a miracle as Indians traditionally took all worthwhile spoils from among the dead. Perhaps they thought Comanche to be as good as dead. Indeed so did the rescuers whose first thought was to put him out of his misery. But the farrier attended his wounds and he was led 15 miles back to the river boat to await evacuation. Bedded under an awning on the aft-deck, the whole ship's company took his welfare to heart. Eventually he arrived at Fort Abraham Lincoln and for nearly a year remained on the sick list, supported by slings. He had received twelve wounds from both bullets and arrows in his flanks, neck and quarters, miraculously all missed vital organs and arteries. He was retired and an order, unique in all the armed forces, went out that he should never be ridden again but would be ceremonially attired and led out for parades. This was complied with up until the last when eventually Comanche died from 'colic and general debility' aged 29 at Fort Riley, Kansas, in 1891. His body was mounted and put on display in the Museum at Kansas University and in 1893 was exhibited at the Chicago World Fair. To this day, he can be seen at Kansas University Natural History Museum.

CIVIL WAR HORSE MEMORIAL

Commissioned by Paul Mellon and created by British sculptress Tessa Pullan, this emotive sculpture honours all the Confederate horses of the Civil War from its permanent position outside the Virginia Historical Society in Richmond, Virginia.

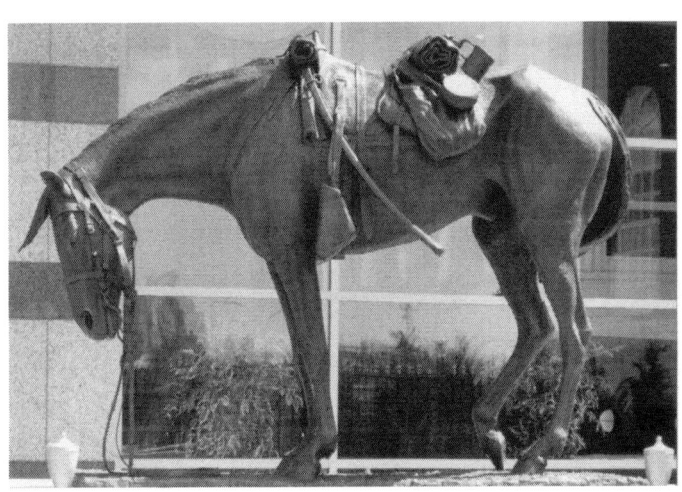

CHIEF

In 1950 the US Army began disbanding the cavalry but compassion was shown to **Chief** and 220 older mounts who were allowed to enjoy retirement in a pasture at Fort Riley, Kansas. Chief was the very last of them and attracted thousands of well-wishers every year until he eventually died at age 36 in 1968. He was buried standing up with full military honours including a colour guard ceremony and band. His grave is on the Cavalry Parade Ground at Fort Riley.

FREDDY

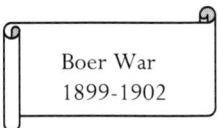

The black gelding **Freddy** was tough. He was part of the Household Cavalry and was shipped out to South Africa. On the day the horses came off the train from Cape Town they were in action at Kimberley at the hottest time of year. Within a few days there was no water at all and over thirty horses were lost from exhaustion and dehydration. Between 11 February and 29 August 1900 Freddy covered 1,780 miles with little rest. He was involved in at least five major actions and was at the relief of Kimberley and the capture of Bloemfontein and Pretoria.

When the Household Cavalry returned home in November 1900 Freddy came with them. The following year he became the leading horse of the Household Cavalry Musical Ride and performed at the Royal Tournament. Queen Alexandra asked why he wore no campaign medal and ordered that he be awarded one immediately, so Freddy was given a medal with five clasps: for Wittenberg, Kimberley, Paarderberg, Direfontein and Transvaal. He carried the standard of the 2nd Life Guards before retiring in 1905. He died in 1911 aged 18 and is buried at the regimental barracks at Windsor.

HORSE MEMORIAL, SOUTH AFRICA

The Horse Memorial honours the 300,000 horses that served and died during the Anglo-Boer War of 1899-1902.

The caring soldier offering his wearied horse some water sits atop a water fountain at the corner of Russell Road and Cape Road in Port Elizabeth, South Africa. The horse is 16.2hh and the soldier is life size. The statue, unveiled 11th February 1905, was designed by Joseph Whitehead and cast in bronze by the Thames Dillon Works in Surrey, UK, and is inscribed:

THE GREATNESS OF A NATION
CONSISTS NOT SO MUCH UPON THE NUMBER OF
ITS PEOPLE
OR THE EXTENT OF ITS TERRITORY
AS IN THE EXTENT AND JUSTICE OF ITS
COMPASSION.

ERECTED BY PUBLIC SUBSCRIPTION
IN RECOGNITION OF THE SERVICES OF THE
GALLANT ANIMALS
WHICH PERISHED IN THE ANGLO BOER WAR
1899-1902

~ ~ ~

The nature of the horse remains unchanged,
whether it carries the saddle of the prince, or
whether it draws the cart of the wagoner. The
noble ones accept the yoke, they serve, but will
never be slaves, for to themselves they can never
be traitors.

H. H. Isenbart, The Kingdom of the Horse

WARRIOR

DIED ...

THIS WHITE GELDING ...
SERVED WITH THE 10TH DRAGOONS IN
IN FRANCE FROM 1914, TO THE END OF
THE WAR. HE TOOK PART IN THE GREAT
FROM 1914 AND WAS WOUNDED IN
THE ADVANCE ON THE AISNE. AFTER
HIS SHRAPNEL HAD BEEN EXTRACTED
HE RETURNED TO DUTY AND DID
SERVICE IN SEVERAL SHARP ACTIONS
UNTIL THE ARMISTICE.
HE WAS PURCHASED BY MISS
HILDA MOORE AND PRESENTED BY
HER TO THE TOWN.

When researching for this particular monument, we
visited the Municipal Golf Course, Southampton,
UK. Earlier the grounds of a mansion, the course, I
had read, was the final resting place of a treasured
charger of the First World War. Arriving at the Club
House we made enquiries - no, there was "no horse

grave here". We moved on to the golf store and asked again. No, "definitely no horse grave here", laughed the manager obviously thinking we were escapees from an asylum. I asked if we could take a look around and he said we could.

A mere thirty feet from his door was the gravestone, right on the side of the access road between the shop and some storage buildings! Set in a horseshoe shaped recess in the hedge within a little triangular garden with primulas in bloom, the site was obviously carefully tended. The gravestone tells **Warrior**'s story:

Warrior
died 22nd August 1935 aged 26 years.
This white gelding, 16hands, served with the
Old Contemptibles in France from 1914 to the
end of the War.
He took part in the Retreat from Mons and
was wounded in the advance on the Aisne.
After the shrapnel had been extracted, he returned to duty
and did service in several further actions until the Armistice.
He was purchased by Miss Hilda Moore and presented by
her to the town.
He at once assumed the chief position in the Police Stud
and became honoured and loved by all, not only for his famous
war record but for his efficacy, intelligence, gentleness
and noble character.

~ ~ ~

BESS

As the personal mount of Colonel Guy Powles, **Bess** saw a great deal of action in the desert campaigns of WW1 and was the only horse to return home to New Zealand at the end of it all. Others had either been detailed to other British units, sold to local traders or destroyed. However, Bess and Colonel Powles came to England where she represented New Zealand at major events. Whilst in England she also played a few chukkas of polo before she and her master returned to New Zealand.

Lt.Col. Powles was out riding one day in October 1934 when his twenty-four year old faithful and never wounded Bess "suddenly decided to lie down and die then and there". Bess was buried where she fell and her proud master erected a memorial for her on the site.

The method of combat was to gallop full tilt to the scene, leap off and fight as infantry. The statue catches the hectic moment of dismount. Bess was never wounded.

On 23rd November 1932 the monument was dedicated in Cairo on behalf of the Australian and New Zealand Governments by Australia's war time Prime Minister W. M. Hughes who was returning from a League of Nations meeting in Europe.

The Cairo unveiling ceremony was broadcast by radio telephone over the 15,000 miles (24,000 kilometres) between Egypt and Australia, the first such direct broadcast between those two countries.

Unfortunately, the original was destroyed in the Suez troubles. A slightly modified copy (pictured) of the original statue now stands at Albany near Perth; and a second copy is in ANZACs Parade, Canberra, Australia.

The bond between human and horse in times of war and peace is perhaps no better portrayed than in the story of Bess and Lt.Col. Powles. There is also a book that recounts Bess's contribution to the war.

Bess's grave site and memorial can be found at Bulls, North Island, New Zealand. The epitaph reads:

BESS
(ZELMA)
SARACEN - MISS JURY

BORN 1910 - MAIN BODY 1914
EGYPT 1915 - SINAI 1916
GERMANY 1919 - ENGLAND 1920
RETURNED NEW ZEALAND
JULY 1920
DIED WHILST ON DUTY
OCTOBER 1934

ERECTED IN HER MEMORY
BY
COL. C.C. POWLES, CMC, QDS, NZSO

The Arabic inscription on the reverse side
of the memorial translates as
'In the Name of the Most High God'

Three sculptors in turn created the statue:
C Webb Gilbert, Paul Montford and Sir Bertram Mackennal.

~ ~ ~

PUTNAM was decorated by General
John J. Pershing as the best artillery horse in the US
Expeditionary Force in France. His own horse was
KIDRON whose skull and skin are in the USA's
Museum of Natural History.

~ ~ ~

WARRIOR

This is another, more famous **Warrior**. This bay horse was bred by the Seely family on the Isle of Wight. He went to the Western Front with his owner and served for four years, proving himself totally indifferent to the bangs and crashes of battle. For the Battle of Ypres Warrior was the mount of the Commander-in-Chief, but then his real master was appointed to command the Canadian Cavalry Brigade of 3,000, and he joined him. The conditions, of course, were appalling and Warrior, like the others, would be exceedingly lucky to have as much as a piece of tarpaulin over his head for protection from the elements, where he waited in deep muddy trenches. Jack Seely was later to describe how horses would sink into the mud and sometimes could not heave themselves out and would die where they fell. When Warrior sank "I would jump off his back and he always managed to struggle out. He was strong." Once when he was stuck a German plane machine-gunned them from on high and Warrior was completely covered with earth – only one forefoot was visible. Fortunately, the men managed to dig him out.

The Canadian soldiers believed "the bullet hasn't been made that can hurt Warrior". While comrades were being shot all around him Warrior would miraculously remain unscathed. He survived being in a house that was blown to bits even though the fallen bricks were piled over him leaving just his nose poking out. He was 'the horse the Germans couldn't kill' according to the *Daily Telegraph*.

Needless to say, his luck and his charisma turned him into a legend and Seely wrote a book about him called "My Horse Warrior". He said "It is a most mysterious thing that this old horse, like some great personality among men, impresses himself upon all whenever he appears; walking about a field by himself or at any other moment, all eyes turn to look at him. His vivid personality was to help me gain the confidence of thousands of brave men, when without him I could never have achieved it."

After starring in the great London Victory March, Warrior went back to his birthplace to retire, but he liked even then to hunt and point-to-point. His life ended in 1941 at age 33, but his memory lives on in a book *My Horse Warrior* by Seely and his paddock is still known as Warrior's Field.

The great horse saw a change in warfare with the arrival of tanks, a change that could only mark an improvement for his fellows.

CAPRICE served with the Royal Hussars. She was the favourite mount of Captain William Eve and shipped with him around the world to various battle sites. She participated near Baghdad, Iraq, in what was to be the final full regimental charge of the British Cavalry – a success but not for Captain Eve. The riderless **Caprice** was seen galloping off into a sandstorm with several bullet wounds in her neck and it was presumed she would never be seen again. However, a year later in Baghdad Caprice whinnied her recognition of her former groom as the Indian cavalry rode through the streets. She was promptly reclaimed by her regiment and shipped home to be cherished by the Eve family. She bred a foal and silver statuettes were made of mare and babe which were given on marriage to officers of the regiment. One is the trophy for a race run at Sandown Park every year, but the original is still the centrepiece of the mess table of the regiment. She is also honoured in a painting by George Paice.

~ ~ ~

PUNCH was totally blind, had been wounded twice and gassed while serving in France, but lived out his life in the care of one of the Homes for old Horses in Britain.

~ ~ ~

KASZTANKA

This chestnut mare was the favourite war horse of Commandant Jozef Pilsudski and became perhaps the most famous horse in Polish culture, admired for her loyalty to her master – indeed she responded only to him and no other.

Marshal Piłsudski rode **Kasztanka** for the last time on November 11th 1927, at the Polish Independence Day parade on Warsaw's Saxon Square (now Piłsudski Square) but ten days later she was to become ill and die. Her hide was mounted and placed in the Belweder Palace museum, but suffered from lack of care and the attention of moths so it was cremated. Her remains were interred in the parkland around the 7th Uhlan Regiment barracks. Her gravestone reads:

Here lies *KASZTANKA*,
favorite combat mare of
Marshal Piłsudski

She has been the subject of many paintings and songs.

~ ~ ~

THE OLD BLACKS

The Old Blacks were a six-horse gun-team of the Royal Horse Artillery, who served together throughout the War, returning to their home barracks in 1919. They were given the distinction of being the team to draw the funeral gun-carriage of the Unknown Warrior to the unveiling of London's Cenotaph on 11th November 1920.

WAR MEMORIAL
Chipilly, France

This incredibly poignant statue (opposite) of an artilleryman trying to comfort his dying horse is in the village of Chipilly on the Somme. Placed in a central position at a road junction with the church nearby, it is a moving commemoration of the losses of both man and horse in that ghastly episode in the First World War.

This monument by H. Gauquie expresses beautifully the anguish of the suffering experienced by both the physically wounded horse and the emotionally wounded soldier. Note the detail of the bridle removed from the head of the horse and hanging on the soldier's right arm. Superb.

War Memorial, Chipilly, France

KITTY

A bay mare whose particular distinction was that she served with one battalion throughout the whole War and never missed a day's duty with the Coldstream Guards. **Kitty** returned home to England and between the ages of eighteen and twenty-two produced three foals. Ultimately she was euthanized at age thirty-one.

DAVID

A wheel horse in a gun-team of 107 Battery, Royal Field Artillery, **David** was already eighteen years old when he went to France in 1914. He wore his South African War ribbons on his bridle and helped pull the guns into place during the whole war, being at nearly every major battle. He was never sick and only slightly wounded once. At the end of the war four officers of the 107 Battery clubbed together and bought him. He lived in peaceful retirement on the Hertfordshire estate of his former commander until he died at thirty years old – apparently the very last surviving horse to have fought throughout the Boer War and WW1.

SANDY was Major General Sir William Throsby Bridges' favourite charger. Bridges served with Australian forces during World War I, and was killed in battle at Gallipoli.

Sandy did not return to Australia with his master's remains. His tour of duty included Gallipoli, Egypt and France. The Minister for Defence called for Sandy's return to Australia in October 1917. Leaving Liverpool, England, nearly one year later, Sandy arrived in Melbourne in 1918. He was officially retired and turned out to graze at the Central Remount Depot in Maribyrnong. Almost five years later, becoming blind and in poor health, Sandy was put to rest in 1923. Of the 136,000 Australian horses sent away to World War I, Sandy was the only one to return home to Australia.

Sandy's head is mounted in a showcase at the Australian War Museum in Canberra but due to deterioration is no longer on public exhibit.

~ ~ ~

DAN was a farm horse from Pevensey, Sussex, who went to war with the lads from his farm and served with them as a troop horse. He returned home to the same farm and lived on well into the 1930s.

Fragments

The very first veterinary clinic in Egypt was founded by the new wife of a British officer residing in Cairo. Being so shock at the site of abandoned war horses in the streets, Dorothy Brooke set up the Old War Horse Memorial Hospital in 1934 to tackle the problem and save the lives of these horses and donkeys. Known now as simply The Brooke, the organisation expanded to tackle cruelty throughout the world.

~ ~ ~

A wounded Northumberland soldier returning from service in WWI where he had served with the Royal Artillery in France, was astonished and delighted to recognise that the horse drawing the milk float in his home town was the very horse that was in his care during his military duties.

~ ~ ~

James Pitcairn, horse artilleryman with the Canadian Army, served in France at Amiens, and in an interview with Veteran Affairs Canada made the poignant observation: "We lost an awful lot of horses ... they couldn't duck ... we saw our own horses get killed. I felt more for a horse than I did for a man for some strange reason, at that time, just at the time ... we know what we are doing, they don't."

William Parr served with the field Artillery in the First Canadian Division, in the First World War, and heard one of the drivers say that should he 'go west' he would like to take his two horses with him. A few days later an exploding shell killed that driver and both his horses. Mr Parr buried the driver with a horse either side of him in the Ypres Salient, Belgium, and wrote a poem on his behalf:

His Two Horses

Oh Lord, to Thee I want to make my prayer,
 My soul is troubled sore from day to day.
 I never had the chance to know Thee Lord,
Nobody ever taught me how to pray.
So if my prayer is not as it should be,
Is not as padre prays on church parade,
Please pardon me, forgive what I've forgot,
For at thy feet my naked soul is laid.
If in the roster kept by Thee above
My name is next to cease this life fatigue,
And I must fall in with my fallen pals
A clean life's page behind I want to leave.
Grant that I die where bursting shrapnel sings.
My team upon a gallop toward the foe,
And when my soul at last reports to Thee,
Please let me take my horses where I go.
If it is true what our old padre says,
That there are horses in the land above,

And there not some spare stalls to hold my two,
My Black, My Brown, the horses that I love
They're only common field artillery plugs,
As I am just a common soldier man,
We've fought and starved together side by side
I'd like to take them with me if I can.
I know my saddle Black is pretty mean
And kicks and bites at everyone but me
Still when I'm with him he is always good
Just let me bring him up for you to see
He'd be ill-treated if I left him here
Be kicked and cursed and starved until he died
Please can't I ride him through the golden streets
The gentle old Brown Off-horse at his side.
They've carried me on many a weary ride,
They've been my pals, my everlasting joy,
I've nursed them both when they were sick
And kept their harness burnished like a toy
I've gone with them into the jaws of death,
Gunners and drivers killed on every trip,
Their panting hides have dripped with mud and sweat,
My horses needed neither spur nor whip.
Oh Lord, if Heaven has not stable room,
With greatest reverence this I'd like to tell,
And if the fiery regions have some stalls,
Then let me ride my horses down in hell.
And when the grand, great, final roll call comes,
To be the first upon parade we'll try.
Oh Lord of All please grant my only prayer,
To take my horses with me when I die.

SGT RECKLESS

The only horse in the US Army to receive a rank. In the Korean War the 4-year-old, 14hh chestnut mare named *Ah-Chim-hal* which meant Flame in the Morning, served with the Marines. Renamed **Reckless** her job was to carry supplies and ammunition to the front line, mostly doing this entirely on her own. One particular day she made 51 trips, walking over 35 miles through paddy fields and up steep mountainous slopes, moving almost five tons of ammunition with enemy fire coming in at her at the rate of 500 rounds per minute. She would also carry wounded soldiers down the mountain to safety, get reloaded with ammo and go back again into the firing. She also provided a shield for Marines who were trying to make their way up to the front line. Reckless was wounded twice and was so beloved by her Marines who took better care of her than they took of themselves, often throwing their flak jackets over her to protect her. They arranged her promotion to Sergeant in 1954. Her Military Decorations included two Purple Hearts, Good Conduct Medal, Presidential Unit Citation with star, National Defense Service Medal, Korean Service Medal, United National Service Medal and Republic of Korea Presidential Unit Citation, all of which were stitched to her red and gold blanket. She came back to the USA with her Marines, had a foal which was named Private First Class Fearless, and enjoyed a peaceful retirement at Camp Pendleton where ultimately she died and is interred. A supporters group run a web site in her name and do all they can to ensure her service is never forgotten. Video footage of Reckless in Korea is available on www.sgtreckless.com.

SEFTON

Although warfare for cavalry was long since over, that didn't protect the horses of the Household Cavalry, who create a much loved spectacle for Londoners, from suffering a car nail bomb attack in 1982 which killed eleven people. Seven horses were also killed outright and others were so severely wounded they died later. **Sefton** had car metal embedded in his neck, one piece severing his jugular vein, five 4-inch nails were implanted in his face and one spiked his back; his stifle and flanks were gored by searing shrapnel; his right eye burned and the cornea damaged. A shirt was stuffed into Sefton's slashed jugular to slow down the spurting blood.

Eight hours of surgery to deal with no less than 38 wounds left Sefton only a 50-50 chance of survival. But he did survive and returned to duty, and the life of a celebrity, taking centre stage at the Horse of the Year show to tumultuous applause, receiving gifts from well wishers and making television appearances. He retired to peaceful pastures in 1984 and ultimately died in 1993. He is buried at the Defence Animal Centre in Melton Mowbray, Leicestershire.

The horses that died were called Cedric, Epaulette, Falcon, Rochester, Waterford, Yeastvite and Zara; of those injured, Echo, Yeti and Sefton recovered.

To this day, each time The Queen's Life Guard pass the spot where the bomb was detonated, they bring their swords down from the "slope" to the "carry" - coupled with an "eyes left" or "eyes right" - as a mark of ongoing tribute.

~ ~ ~

A Soldier's Kiss

by Henry Chappell

Only a dying horse! pull off the gear,
And slip the needless bit from frothing jaws,
Drag it aside there, leaving the road way clear,
The battery thunders on with scarce a pause.
Prone by the shell-swept highway there it lies
With quivering limbs, as fast the life-tide fails,
Dark films are closing o'er the faithful eyes
That mutely plead for aid where none avails.
Onward the battery rolls, but one there speeds
Needlessly of comrades voice or bursting shell,
Back to the wounded friend who lonely bleeds
Beside the stony highway where he fell.
Only a dying horse! he swiftly kneels,
Lifts the limp head and hears the shivering sigh
Kisses his friend, while down his cheek there steals
Sweet pity's tear, "Goodbye old man, Goodbye".
No honours wait him, medal, badge or star,
Though scarce could war a kindlier deed unfold;
He bears within his breast, more precious far
Beyond the gift of kings, a heart of gold.

~ ~ ~

THE LAST POST

The record of the contribution of individual horses and horses in general to humanity's wars is, for the most part, being carefully preserved in one form or another — statues, grave markers, poetry, paintings, songs, artefacts, etc. But these memorials are scattered and often obscure, or not made comprehensible to the casual observer. I hope this little volume will go some way towards creating a central resource for the widest possible audience to easily access the incredible biographies of our equine war heroes and illustrate the emotional involvement of those who felt the horses' pumping hearts.

During the research and writing I have had the privilege of speaking with some warm and inspirational people who have demonstrated a real pride and caring for individual war horses of the past. They have lifted my spirits during some very sad and emotional research campaigns into the historical record of the horses who have fought our battles.

~ ~ ~

Tessa Pullan's Civil War Horse, Richmond, Virginia

ACKNOWLEDGEMENTS

Australian War Museum, Canberra
Brereton, J.M.: *The Horse in War*
Clutton-Brock, Juliet: *Horse Power*
Deene Park
HathiTrust.org (*The Gentleman's Magazine*)
Hoare, Richard
New Zealand Mounted Rifles Association
Maidstone Museum
Royal Armoury, Stockholm, Sweden
M Stowe
Wear, Terri A: *The Horse's Name Was ...*
Westphal, M
www.GreatBattles co.uk.

Green, Jane A - the majority of the pictures inc covers.
Richard Barnes - p.33
Genghis Khan Park, Mongolia - p.12
Goellnitz,Jennifer - p.65
Hafer, Margi - p.64
Halling, Philip - p.42
Hargrave, Simon and Laura e - p.27 and 28
House, C - p.17
Lee Brauer Photography Inc - p.97
Legg, Joanna (www.greatwars.co.uk) p.85
Lexington History Museum, Kentucky – p.54
Darren Wyn Rees - p.43
Marine Corps, USA - p.92
Schmidt, Goran - p.16
Thomas, R - p.77
US Cavalry Museum, Fort Riley - 71
Virginia Military Institute - p.56

GLOSSARY

Hand: the measuring unit of a horse's height. A hand is equal to four inches. A 15.2hh horse is therefore 5ft 2inches tall, the measurement being taken from the ground to the withers (the point where the neck joins the shoulders).

Bay: colour of horse which is basically a dark brown body with black mane and tail.

Bridle: the leather strapping used on a horse's head for control and steering purposes, both in riding and driving. It holds the metal bit in place in the horse's mouth to which the reins are attached.

Chestnut: A reddish brown body with similar coloured mane and tail. This is quite a wide range of colours from the shade of digestive biscuits to a deep orangey red.

Drum Horse: Drums were used to cause fear in the enemy at the same time inspiring the courage of comrades. While the drums rolled the soldiers knew that the Colour (regimental banner) was still flying. The drums were also used to transmit orders from the CO during battle. Drum horses carried two huge kettle drums, plus their own equipment and the drumsman and needed to be stoic and strong; they are still used for Parade purposes.

Flea-bitten Gray: a colour that is basically grey but with flecks of darker hair scattered all over the body.

Forage: hay or grass or sometimes straw fed to horses who all require to eat large amounts of fibre in order to keep their digestive systems working correctly.

Gait: the gaits of a horse are walk, trot and canter; the smooth gait referred to often in the USA section is the extra gait offered by some horses who retain an ancient genetic heritage. This is where the horse can switch from a regular two beat lateral or diagonal gait, to a smooth four-beat gait, where each foot strikes the ground independently not as a pair, offering a very smooth glide to his rider.

Palfrey: easy-gaited (see Gait above) riding horse favoured in the UK's Middle Ages by the nobility and clerics.

Pinto: a coat of brown/black and white patches.

Point-to-Point: a horse race over 18 birch brush fences which is restricted to horses and jockeys that have hunted at least four times in the preceding season. Often used as a 'training ground' for young horses destined for the big National Hunt races (e.g. The Grand National).

Reins: Narrow lines of leather running from the horse's bit to the rider's hands (known as 'lines' in driving).

Riderless Horse: a custom involving the horse of the deceased following the coffin in the funeral cortege – preferably the deceased's own horse where possible.

Shabraque: the colourful stylish cloth placed under a horse's saddle and draping slightly down his sides – particularly in French cavalry.

Socks: white markings on the legs upward from hoof to first joint

Stifle: the joint at the top of each back leg that bends forward like a knee.

Whinny: the sound a horse makes in friendly communication either with other horses or with people. Although slightly different in meaning, the whinny is sometimes called a whicker.

'Nothing is more sacred as the bond between a horse and a rider. No other creature can ever become so emotionally close to a human as a horse. When a horse dies, the memory lives on, because an enormous part of his owner's heart, soul, and the very existence dies also.'

S M Thorn